# Farm Animals

# Sheep

Rachael Bell

Heinemann
LIBRARY

The author wishes to thank Tom Clifford for giving his time and insight.

First published in Great Britain by Heinemann Library
Halley Court, Jordan Hill, Oxford OX2 8EJ,
a division of Reed Educational and Professional Publishing Ltd.
Heinemann is a registered trademark of Reed Educational & Professional Publishing Limited.

OXFORD MELBOURNE AUCKLAND
JOHANNESBURG BLANTYRE GABORONE
IBADAN PORTSMOUTH NH (USA) CHICAGO

Designed by AMR
Originated by Ambassador Litho Ltd
Printed in Hong Kong/China

04 03 02 01 00
10 9 8 7 6 5 4 3 2 1

ISBN 0 431 10081 0

**British Library Cataloguing in Publication Data**
Bell, Rachael, 1972–
  Sheep. – (Farm animals)
  1.Sheep – Juvenile literature
  I.Title
  636.3

**Acknowledgements**
The Publishers would like to thank the following for permission to reproduce photographs:
Agripicture p 21/Peter Dean; J Allan Cash Ltd, p 27; Anthony Blake Photo Library p 23/Sue Atkinson; Bruce Coleman pp 8/Jorg & Petra Wegner, 18/Stephen Bond; Farmers Weekly Picture Library pp 11, 13, 19; Holt Studios pp 4 l/Richard Anthony, 12 & 14/Wayne Hutchinson, 15/Primrose Peacock, 24/Gordon Roberts; Chris Honeywell p 25; Images of Nature/FLPA pp 4 r/Tony Hamblin, 5/I. Lee Rue, 6/Derek A. Robinson, 16/Peter Dean, 17/M. J. Thomas, 20/Peter Dean; Martin Sookias, p 22; Lynn M Stone pp 9, 10, 28; Tony Stone Images pp 7/Philip H. Coblentz, 26/Anthony Cassidy, 29/David Woodfall.

Cover photograph reproduced with permission of NHPA.

Our thanks to Tony Prior, Bowers Farm, Wantage, Oxon, for his comments in the preparation of this book.

Every effort has been made to contact copyright holders of any material reproduced in this book. Any omissions will be rectified in subsequent printings if notice is given to the Publisher.

For more information about Heinemann Library books, or to order, please phone 01865 888066, or send a fax to 01865 314091. You can visit our web site at www.heinemann.co.uk

# Contents

Words in bold **like this** are explained
in the Glossary.

# Sheep relatives

Most sheep are white, but they can also be black or dark brown. Their coats may be long and curly or short and smooth. However they look, they all make a deep 'baa' noise!

Farmers choose sheep that suit where they live, so most sheep in one area look the same. Some sheep live wild, like this Bighorn sheep in North America.

# Welcome to the sheep farm

On this farm, the farmer keeps many sheep. He also has a sheep-dog. The sheep-dog is a working animal and is kept outside in the farmyard.

Most of the land on the farm is used
for **grazing** the sheep. The rest is used
for **crops** like wheat and oats. These
are turned into bread or breakfast
**cereal**. The **hay** is sold as horse food.

# Meet the sheep

tail

udder

The **female** sheep is called a **ewe**.
Ewes have up to three lambs a year.
They take good care of the lambs.
Two lambs can drink milk from their
mother at the same time.

eye    horn

jaw    hoof

The **male** sheep is called a ram. Some rams have horns. They can use them to fight off other rams and **protect** the ewes.

# Meet the baby sheep

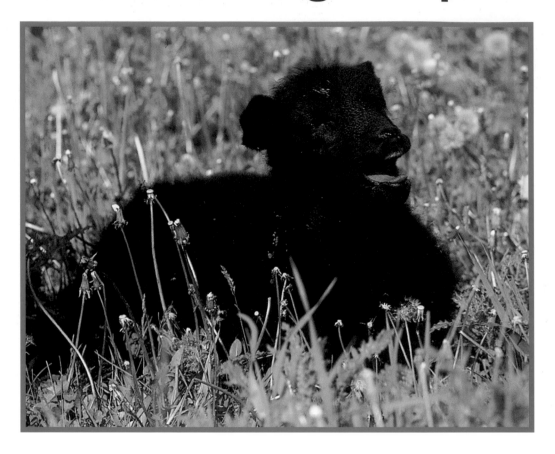

Baby sheep are called lambs. They can walk within minutes of being born. Lambs make a high-sounding noise, called bleating.

When lambs are very young, they feed on milk from their mother. Before long, the lambs start to eat grass and other food.

# Where do sheep live?

Sheep spend most of their life outdoors. They are very tough animals. A sheep's thick **fleece** keeps it warm, even in freezing weather.

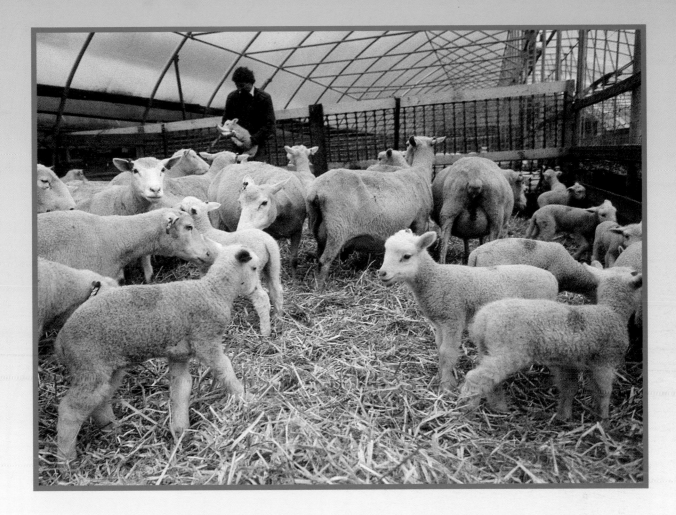

At **lambing time**, most sheep are kept in a barn with deep **straw** on the floor. The **ewe** and her lambs go outside again when the lambs are about three weeks old.

# What do sheep eat?

teeth in bottom jaw

pad in top of mouth

Sheep's mouths are made for nibbling short grass. They bite off grass between their bottom front teeth and upper **pad**, then swallow it. Later they **chew the cud** between their back teeth.

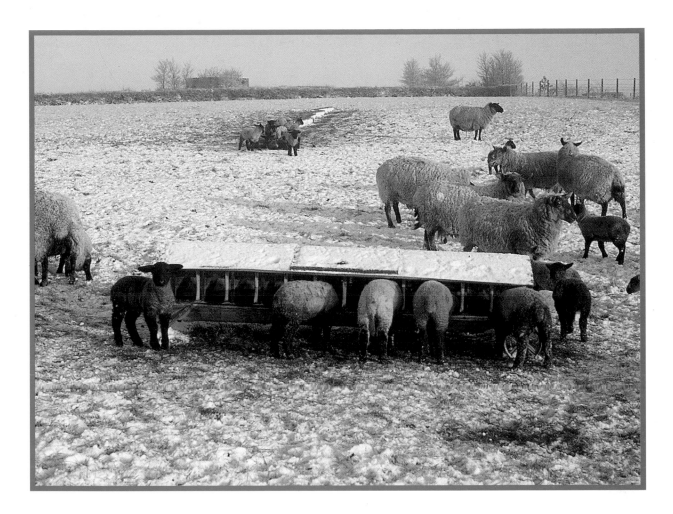

In winter when the grass stops growing quickly, sheep eat **hay** and **ewe** nuts. Ewe nuts are made from **cereals**, like your breakfast food. They drink water from **troughs** all year round.

# How do sheep stay healthy?

Sheep catch **diseases** and **parasites** very easily. They get them from each other and from the ground. The best way to keep sheep healthy is to make sure they only have fresh grass.

Farmers take good care of their sheep. They dip the sheep in a special liquid to kill any parasites. They also give the sheep **injections** against diseases.

# How do sheep sleep?

As it gets dark, the sheep gather together. They find a sheltered area and lie down with their backs to the wind.

Sheep sleep with their eyes closed. If
you disturb them, they wake up and
run off. Sometimes they **graze** too,
but they soon lie down again to rest.

# Who looks after the sheep?

The **shepherd** checks the sheep every day in the field with his sheep-dog. The dog runs around the sheep to collect them up and move them to the next field.

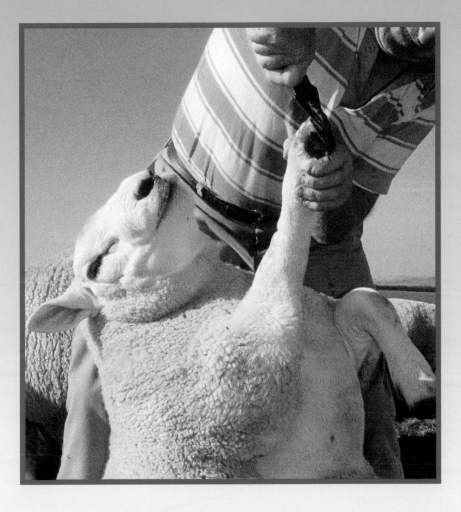

The farmer and his shepherd look
after the **ewes** when they are inside.
Sometimes they trim the sheep's
**hooves** – a bit like cutting your nails!

# What are sheep kept for?

Most farms keep sheep for their
meat. The meat from sheep is called
lamb. It can be used in many
different dishes.

The main cuts of meat from a lamb
are the shoulder, leg or lamb chop.
This is a roast leg of lamb.

# What else are sheep kept for?

Sheep are also kept for their wool. A sheep's **fleece** is **sheared** off – a bit like having a hair cut. The fleece is sent to a factory to be cleaned and spun into wool.

Some farms also keep sheep for their creamy milk. They make special cheeses and yoghurt from it. Roquefort is a famous blue cheese made from **ewes'** milk.

# Other kinds of sheep farm

In some parts of the world, farmers keep sheep high up in the mountains. The **shepherd** moves around with his sheep.

In Australia, big sheep farms are called sheep stations. They have many thousands of sheep. The sheep are left alone for most of the year, until they are rounded up for market.

# Fact file

 Sheep prefer being together in a **flock**. If one sheep moves, the others follow it.

 Lambs are born with eight **milk teeth**. Every year, two of their milk teeth fall out and are replaced by adult teeth. After only a few years these adult teeth start to fall out.

 When a lamb is about one day old, the farmer puts a tight rubber ring on its tail. This makes the tail fall off. It does not hurt the lamb and stops it getting dirty under the tail.

Sometimes a farmer needs a **ewe** to feed a lamb that is not her own. He holds the lamb where the ewe cannot see or smell it. Soon she gets used to the new lamb and lets it feed from her. If this does not work, the farmer's family feed the lamb from a bottle, just like a baby!

 Sheep's **fleeces** have been used for over 3000 years to make wool. Most families had a spinning wheel to turn the fleece into wool.

# Glossary

| | |
|---|---|
| **cereals** | wheat, oats and barley, often made into breakfast food |
| **chew the cud** | bring food back up into the mouth from the stomach, to chew it again |
| **crops** | plants that the farmer grows in his fields |
| **diseases** | illnesses |
| **ewe** | female or mother sheep |
| **female** | the girl or mother |
| **fleece** | sheep's coat of wool |
| **flock** | group of sheep that live together |
| **graze** | eat grass in a field |
| **hay** | cut and dried grass |
| **hooves** | the hard pads of the sheep's feet |
| **injections** | special medicines which are given through a needle |
| **lambing time** | when the lambs are born |
| **male** | the boy or father |
| **milk teeth** | the first teeth |
| **pad** | hard area in sheep's mouth |

| | |
|---|---|
| **parasites** | little animals that live on bigger animals and usually harm them |
| **protect** | keep safe |
| **sheared** | how the fleece of a sheep is cut off in one bundle |
| **shepherd** | man or woman who looks after sheep |
| **straw** | thick, dried stalks from crops |
| **trough** | food or water container for animals |
| **udder** | the sheep's milk bag |

# More books to read

## Story books

*I love Animals*, Walker Books
*Picnic Farm*, Macmillan
*Over in the Meadow*, Walker Books

## Information books

*Animal Young – Mammals*, Heinemann Library
*Images – On the Farm*, Heinemann Library
*The Farming Year, Autumn, Winter, Spring, Summer*,
   Wayland
*Mealtimes – Evening Meals Around the World*, Wayland

# Index